Beetles

Macdonald

About Macdonald Starters

Macdonald Starters are vocabulary controlled information books for young children. More than ninety per cent of the words in the text will be in the reading vocabulary of the vast majority of young readers. Word and sentence length have also been carefully controlled.

Key new words associated with the topic of each book are repeated with picture explanations in the Starters dictionary at the end. The dictionary can also be used as an index for teaching children to look things up.

Teachers and experts have been consulted on the content and accuracy of the books.

A MACDONALD BOOK

© Macdonald & Co (Publishers) Ltd 1974

First published in
Great Britain in 1974

This edition first published in
Great Britain in 1986

British Library Cataloguing in Publication Data
Ferguson, Diana
Beetles. – (Starters)
  1. Readers – 1950 –
  I. Title   II. Corbett, Grahame
  428.6   PE1119

  ISBN 0-356-04635-4
  ISBN 0-356-11496-1 Pbk

Printed and bound in Great Britain by
Purnell & Sons (Book Production) Ltd,
Paulton, Bristol

Published by Macdonald & Co (Publishers) Ltd
Maxwell House
74 Worship Street
London EC2A 2EN

Members of BPCC plc

Illustrator: Grahame Corbett

Here is a beetle.
It has crawled out from under a stone.

1

A beetle is an insect.
It has six legs.

2

Most beetles have wings.
The wing covers protect the wings.
The wing covers lift up
when beetles fly.

3

Beetles lay eggs.
The eggs hatch into larvae
like these.

4

Later the larvae change into beetles.
Some larvae change into beetles
under the ground.

5

These burying beetles have found
a dead rat.
They will bury the rat.

6

Then they will lay their eggs
on the rat.

These scarab beetles
have made a ball out of dung.
They will lay their eggs in it.

8

The larvae of the tiger beetle
look like this.
They hide in holes.
They eat any insect that comes near.

Stag beetles live on tree trunks.
The males have large jaws.

10

Stag beetles fly about
on summer evenings.
These are flying round a light.

Here are some longhorn beetles.
They eat very little food.
But they sometimes eat pollen
from flowers.

Many of these potato plants
are dying.
Colorado beetles have eaten
all the leaves.

Here is a diving beetle.
It goes under water
taking air under its wings.
14

These are whirlygig beetles.
They go round and round
on top of the water.

These ants are trying to kill
a bombardier beetle.
The beetle squirts out some poison.
Some of the ants die.
16

This is a devil's coach-horse.
It has a sharp bite.
It stands up like this
when it is afraid.

Birds do not eat ladybirds.
Ladybirds do not taste nice.
The birds know this
from the colours of the ladybirds.
18

Flea beetles can jump.
They jump away from danger.

Fireflies are beetles.
You can see them in the dark.

20

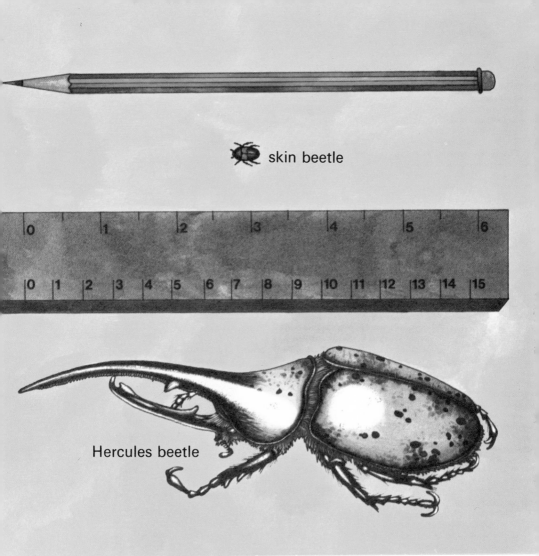

skin beetle

Hercules beetle

There are many different kinds
of beetles.
Here is one of the biggest
and one of the smallest.

This man lived in Egypt long ago.
His ring is shaped like a scarab beetle.

22

Starter's **Beetles** words

tone
(page 1)

wings
(page 3)

egs
(page 2)

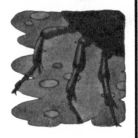

wing
covers
(page 3)

abdomen
(page 2)

eggs
(page 4)

head
(page 2)

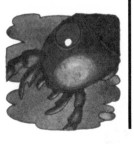

larvae
(page 4)

burying beetle
(page 6)

rat
(page 6)

scarab beetle
(page 8)

stag beetle
(page 10)

jaws
(page 10)

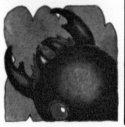

light
(page 11)

longhorn beetle
(page 12)

flower
(page 12)

potato plant
(page 13)

Colorado beetle
(page 13)

diving
beetle
(page 14)

flea
beetle
(page 19)

whirlygig
beetle
(page 15)

fireflies
(page 20)

ants
(page 16)

skin
beetle
(page 21)

birds
(page 18)

Hercules
beetle
(page 21)

ladybird
(page 18)

ring
(page 22)